COLLECTED FATHER

poems by

John Pijewski

Finishing Line Press
Georgetown, Kentucky

COLLECTED FATHER

Copyright © 2026 by John Pijewski
ISBN 979-8-89990-310-6 First Edition
All rights reserved under International and Pan-American Copyright Conventions. No part of this book may be reproduced in any manner whatsoever without written permission from the publisher, except in the case of brief quotations embodied in critical articles and reviews.

ACKNOWLEDGMENTS

Publisher: Leah Huete de Maines
Editor: Christen Kincaid
Cover Art: John O'Reilly
Author Photo: Carol Lynn Alpert
Cover Design: Cover Design: Elizabeth Maines McCleavy

Order online: www.finishinglinepress.com
        also available on amazon.com

Author inquiries and mail orders:
Finishing Line Press
PO Box 1626
Georgetown, Kentucky 40324
USA

Contents

ONE

His First One 1
Chores 3
Farm 4
The World 5
Birthing 7
Three Years 8
Eyes Closed 13
His Body 15
Death 16

TWO

As If My Father's Life Was His 19
Call It Home 20
Haircut 22
Education 23
Pickles and Herring 24
A Polish Summer 25
New Testament 27
Eviction 28
Songbird 30
My Brother's First Communion Photo 33
Durak 36
His Lost Polish Son 37
Soup 38
Exquisite 41

THREE

Ritual 45
Gifts 46
Sweet Nothings 47
Satan 49
Lucky 50
Handyman 51
Kiki 55
Dancing with My Father 56
Strongman 57
The Connoisseur of Cow Manure 58

Something	59
Intimacy	60
Father's Day	61
Friday Nights	62
Winter Father	64

FOUR

Brief World	67
Birdcalls	68
Bruised Light	69
Father's Garden	70
Ode to a Sofa	71
A Lifetime	73
His Last Job	74
The Past	77
Pijewski & Sons	79
1001 Polish Nights	81
Ziggy's Body	82
Last Time	86
The Wake	88

FIVE

Coffin	91
Taking Out the Trash: ONE	92
Son of Dracula	93
The Brothers Pijewski	95
Dead Father	96
Someone's Father	99
Homecoming	100
Patrimony	101
Taking Out the Trash: TWO	102
Scenes with my Father	103

*In memory of my brother Jerzy (Jurek) Pijewski (1950—2010)
who, in the 3rd grade, insisted he be called George.*

ONE

His First One

Drunk again. This time, for once, he spilled a story.
That Sunday he cast his hook with twine, filched

from his mother, that he lashed to a branch he'd
severed from a pond side birch. The perch

refusing to bite. A grayish thing—an archipelago
of tiny islands—floating in pond center.

Flour sack or pillow? A trinity of dead ducks?
His cork bobble wouldn't cast close enough.

Only when he knotted a nail to the twine did
the hook come close. Devolving into a game. Toss,

hand pull the line. Keep tossing. Until he snagged
the thing, tugged the water-logged whatever-it-was

slowly to shore. So heavy it could be a log. Or
valise crammed with hundreds of soggy banknotes.

Then recognized it, stopped hauling. A dead child
face down. Naked, bloated, discolored. The stench

crawling into his brain. He vomited that morning's
milk and bread. Someone his age. Boy or girl,

he couldn't tell. He felt his intestines liquefy.
The body so gruesome all he could do was stare

and stare. A murder of crows clustered in a tree
were cawing, accusing him. Do something.

But what could a boy do? He hacked at the twine.
Sacrificed his only fishing hook. Found a stick,

poked the child's corpse away from shore. Then
three slow kilometers back home. He wished

the world would disappear. He wouldn't tell anyone.
Couldn't tell anyone. For sure he'd get a father

beating that'd have him oozing blood. For months
no word of a missing child. How could anyone

ever lose a child? He imagined the body sinking
into mud as fish feed. That was his first dead body.

His second was his mother who died in the fall.
And then, during the war, there were plenty more.

Chores

After chores my father, age six, and his older brother
stripped out of their sweaty, dirty tatters,

washed themselves at the tin tub with rainwater
drained off the roof. They wiped each other's back

careful not to distress their welts and scabs.
Then lay shirtless on their stomachs for the breeze

to cool their skin. My father studied his brother's back,
which must be exactly like his own, looking

just like their empty fields ravaged last winter,
then ploughed by their father this past spring.

Farm

After work broke, Tadek lugged
scuttles of rocks sieved from the field,

poured them into growing piles. Last year
he'd finished school at age twelve.

He twisted heads off chickens, gutted
his first pig. He couldn't leave Srebrenica

after his brother Francisek disappeared.
No mystery there. The constant sparks

with their boozy father. Tadek now had
the straw mattress to himself, wore clothes

Francisek left behind. There were three pigs.
Two cows. An aging horse. Two drunken

uncles. Tadek's mother dead four years.
Storage bins for potatoes, cabbages, beets,

nearly empty. If his father could distill
vodka from rocks, they'd be rich.

The World

At the pond Tadek sees three boys peppering
the water's lazy surface with a spray of rocks,

waking the pond in August heat. They say they
walked from three villages away to swim here.

They shuck their clothes, snap birch branches
to smack each other until they're yelping and

charging into the pond. Tadek feels himself
melting, weightless. The boys are splashing,

jeering, goading him to join their horseplay.
Tadek feels he's drifting away. He unravels

half the truth—he doesn't know how to swim.
Like drunken hawks the boys screech and swoop

ashore. When their startling white bodies emerge
from water, Tadek feels himself lifting higher.

The three boys wrestle him to the ground,
drag him waterward, heave him into the pond;

keep nudging his thrashing body farther out.
He found a child's swollen corpse floating here

a few years ago, discolored, decomposing, sex
unrecognizable; its putrid stench still crawling

inside his brain. He feels the dead child's hands
grabbing his feet, pulling him under. He thinks

he'll sink into the sucking ooze of muddy
sediment, but he starts screaming, climbing

the water furiously. The boys stop laughing.
Their slippery eel-bodies are grappling

a frantic Tadek to haul him to shore.
Back on pond bank, he's shaking and gasping,

puking the bilge of pond water, his belly
bloated, lungs burning, heart about to explode.

These three skinny, naked boys are stunned
silent. Standing over Tadek. Three boys with

no idea what to do. They don't know it yet,
but they've just invented the world.

Birthing

The midwife arrived to find
Stefania, seven months

pregnant, already dead.
She peeled back layers

of blood-soaked rags,
inserted her fist to extract

the warm corpse of a girl
she swaddled in a towel

next to mother. The priest
summoned. Chairs and stools

arranged for the vigil.
Candles burning when Tadek

returned from his weekly
Saturday night in the village

to his father's epic cursing.
Son Zdzislaw, already three,

wailing in his basket crib.
My future father blundered

into the room, wildly drunk,
waving off his father,

stumbling in his shoes,
barging into the bedroom,

climbing into bed with
his wife and daughter.

Three Years

Bunks were stacked three tiers high. Three inmates to each tier. More than two hundred inmates in his block. Each one a stinking farm animal.

Just days in the camp, already starving, all they talked about were the sausages, dumplings, poppy seed pastries they'd eaten at home. They stopped when their digestive juices began eating the lining of their empty stomachs.

They worked 12 hours each day for 13 days. Then one day off.

The bread contained sawdust, snips of brown grass, crushed leaves, dead insects. He couldn't eat it fast enough.

Breathing the coal dust and grit in the mine gave him a hacking cough. At day's end his mouth and teeth ached as if he'd been chewing sand.

Roll calls took place every morning and evening. In heat, rain, cold, fog, mud, snow. You had to stand at attention until each inmate was accounted for.

He watched Koba beat Brunek unconscious with an iron pipe because his portion of stale bread was larger, then saw Koba steal the shoes from Brunek's feet. When a *kapo* killed Koba months later my father took his shoes.

If a horse died in camp the potato peel soup contained a few slivers of meat.

He saw Pawel didn't have enough strength to visit the latrine at night. He also saw the guard watching Pawel squatting in the corner. The next day Pawel was gone.

The three men who collapsed in the coal mine died. Their bodies were propped sitting against the rock wall, heads leaning forward, as if napping.

Too exhausted, too hungry to sleep, he hugged his bunkmate Tomasz for warmth. He listened to the room of men snoring and farting, some fucking as quietly as they could.

Public beatings occurred after evening roll call. An inmate played an accordion while another inmate was stripped, tied to a post and whipped by a *kapo*. You had to stand at attention. Afterwards some of the men hummed the accordion tune.

When drunk, a guard told the inmates the plan was to work them to death.

When he couldn't fall asleep he felt a razor-sharp emptiness that was his body craving animal fat. He remembered, as a boy, sopping rye bread in bacon drippings in a still warm frying pan.

Some of the men did favors for the *kapos* for a boiled beet or potato. Special favors earned a sausage.

He crawled over Julek to use the latrine at night. In the morning Tomasz helped him carry Julek's corpse outside for roll call. They cleaned the blood and shit in the bunk with straw.

The worst *kapos* were Russian criminals. When angry or drunk, they administered beatings over the most trivial, or imaginary, infractions. You learned to look away.

Even when the soup was rancid or the bread stale he always wished there was more.

The itching from lice bites never went away.

Often he wondered how he would he die. From the hunger, exhaustion, a *kapo's* anger, typhus, a mine accident, the freezing cold, or the boredom?

When someone stole his tin bowl, the food server ladled the watery cabbage soup into his cupped hands.

He still worked when he was sick. He bribed the *kapo* to cut him some slack, provided info about certain men dealing contraband.

When he opened the door to the latrine, the stench lifted him off his feet.

He'd been punched, kicked, whipped, spat on, beaten with a club, knocked to the ground, had shit thrown at him, been left standing overnight up to his neck in a mud hole. He was once pushed into a pit with corpses. Someone's idea of a joke.

In his dream it was raining soup. He hauled himself outside, dropped on his hands and knees to slurp from every puddle.

He saw Stefan attack a guard with a shovel. A quick way to commit suicide.

Those long days lugging countless bricks from a train onto trucks deep into the night. He could only nibble at his rye bread as if he was a mouse.

There were some evenings he drank contraband vodka that a guard sold for an exorbitant price. He never got as drunk as he wanted.

An officer reprimanded the *kapos*. If you want to knock out inmates' teeth, target the older men. The younger ones have too much work in them to waste.

So his feet wouldn't freeze he wrapped them in rags before putting on his shoes. When the rags became frayed and useless, he shredded them to add to his soup.

Using a two-man saw he downed pine trees with Felek. Against the winter chill they wore long black overcoats that swirled into a flurry of crows lifting into the air.

On lunch break in the forest he scraped the softer bark from saplings with a rock's sharp edge, filling his pockets to share with friends later.

Evening roll call was worse than morning roll call. You had to stand at attention when all you wanted was to lie down in the mud or dirty snow and sleep.

At night they sometimes played a card game where the loser had water poured into his shoes.

They all stood naked in the rain when their barrack was fumigated for lice.

He saw his bunkmate Tomasz hanging by a belt from a beam in the washroom, trousers fallen down his legs. He thought Tomasz was a side of beef about to be butchered.

There were days when everything he looked at reminded him of food—doors, wooden boards, piles of clothing, bricks, shovels, shoes. Especially shoes.

His shirt and trousers hung on him as if he was a clothesline.

He never imagined the things he'd eat in camp. Cardboard, a cotton cap, paper, an officer's napkin left out in the rain, rats slow-cooked on the coal stove, a wedge of shoe leather he'd cut into four smaller pieces. He chewed each piece for an hour before it was soft enough to swallow.

When the sirens sounded before dawn, he had to dig himself out of his grave.

Those good days on farm detail. Extra armed guards posted so the inmates wouldn't steal potatoes and beets. He decapitated heads of cabbage with a scythe.

He was certain he saw the Virgin Mary appear in the barbed wire outside his barrack.

Some of the inmates sucked on buttons or pebbles for hours. They looked as if they were toothless, mumbling prayers.

When he was in the labor camp long enough, he survived by blocking out everything around him. Ignoring the bitter humor, cursing, arguments, beatings, and deaths. He learned to focus on single moments as they occurred—

Jabbing a shovel into the ground.

Running his tongue slowly over his cracked lips.

Straining his back to lift his end of a drainage pipe.

Hearing the hollow clinking when he shoveled coal on top of coal.

Smelling his rancid clothes before putting them on.

Feeling that ominous gurgling in his stomach.

Wrapping the broken blisters on his hands and feet with rags.

At night dropping onto his scratchy straw bedding.

Closing his eyes.

Eyes Closed

Their one day off every two weeks. No trees to shield
the strict rows of barracks in camp. Such a relief to

burrow himself in the shade wedged between barracks
beyond the sight of metal fencing crowned with curls

of barbed wire. The sliver of sky above is washed-out
pale blue with wisps of clouds like a white sheet

shredding. If he closes his eyes he can concentrate on
the distant commotion of men playing soccer in

the camp's courtyard and imagine he's back in…..
But he resists the pull of memory. With eyes closed

the darkness is total joy. A warm, humid breeze
from the south. Beyond the fence the fields are

blessed with crops. If only he could be assigned to
farm detail. Beyond the crops there's the barricade

of the forest's edge, but it might as well be France,
a country he knows he'll never see. He feels hunger

most when he's not consumed by work. Hunger is
a knife scraping his stomach lining, sharpening all

his senses, thinning the air into ether, spinning him
light-headed and dizzy, stoking energy he's learned

not to trust, so he struggles to lie still, fights the urge
to rise and walk. Stillness and inertia a victory.

Tonight, as usual, there'll be thin soup with ghosts
of cabbage and carrots, a slice of black bread. Then

they'll settle into playing cards. As much as they
resist, they'll surrender to the trap of discussing

favorite meals their wives and mothers cooked.
How tall the stalks of rye would be right now.

How heads of cabbage were lopped off with scythes,
packed into storage. Feeding the pig if you were lucky

to have one. How he loved to sink his potato spade
into the ground, as if digging for treasure.

His Body

My father lay on his back, eyes closed, in a thin
patch of weeds behind the camp infirmary, hidden

from the fence capped with coils of barbed wire.
He waited here for her to sit beside him, to bring

that warm scent of baking apples with her.
She always began with a soft, slow caressing

of her fingertips across his forehead. Brushing
his stubbled skull and cheeks. Tracing the whorls

of his ears, the strong line of his nose. Grazing
fingers across his eyelids, through his eyebrows.

Her sighs almost lulling him to sleep. Never
saying a single word. Saving his lips for last,

her touch balm soothing their cracked, pallid
pink. Watching how her son's chest rose and

fell slowly. Praying that her grief wouldn't
transfigure his body into cold, carved marble.

Death

My father didn't want to die.
Then he died so many times,

he became accustomed to it.
Death listened to what my father said,

began slicing my father's bread for him,
pouring his vodka.

Death whispered
flattering things into his ear.

Death made him feel respected,
cherished. Death was always there,

warm and naked, eager to have
my father enter his bed.

TWO

As If My Father's Life Was His

World War I scrubbed his childhood with dirt
on a Polish farm. His father knotted him

like a rope. Nine when his mother died.
Two older brothers who kicked him around.

Farm work fulltime at age 12. He recited
wedding vows with a teenage farm girl,

then fell down drunk. At 22, father to a son.
Poland surrendered, and his wife died

birthing a daughter. Who also died.
Sent to a Nazi labor camp, he left his son

in the mud on his father's farm. Death,
his best buddy during the war. After the war

he was buried in a D.P. camp's bureaucracy.
He married my future mother who birthed him

a stillborn daughter. Five long years to find
a country, any country, to accept them

as war refugees. Age 36, he entered America
with a wife, an infant son who'd be my brother.

The present is built on top of memories
that cloud the future.

I was born 18 months later in Boston.
As if this is when my life began.

Call It Home

That brick and stone village, Boston's West End,
slated for demolition. Century-old architecture

as tenement slum. Cooking odors stewing ripe,
rank, and greasy. Foreign languages scurrying

like rodents and roaches. Rents halved so tenants
would stay. Landlords cannibalizing what they

could sell for scrap---pipes and wires wrenched
from walls; doorknobs, window-sash weights.

Stores were vacant, front doors boarded up.
The silence of derelict streets. Dogs scavenging

cobbled alleys. From our rear fire escape I peered
through broken windows into empty buildings.

As if the German army had swept through,
arrested everyone. Except for our family.

We lived in this wasteland for weeks plodding
far for food. So close to my father's meat-packing

plant on the waterfront, Boston Sausage; close
to parks along the Charles, downtown shopping.

He held out until a towering crane with a slow-
swaying wrecking ball Godzilla-ed our street.

A month later, he Sunday-strolled us through
a war zone to where our building once stood,

the street sprawled like a ravaged corpse. Father
wouldn't let us climb piles of toppled brick walls,

wooden timbers, shattered glass, scalps of plaster
clumps. I watched a dog sniffing debris to find

the granite corner he'd always pissed on.
History erasing my father's world yet again.

Load whatever fits into a wobbling wooden cart,
wheel the cart to some distant hole. Call it home.

Haircut

My father dropped me into the wooden chair
he'd dragged under the kitchen's bare bulb.

I wanted hair I could comb but he bristled,
insisted on a skull cut because he'd razor-shaved

the heads in his barrack at the labor camp.
I was the new inmate prepped to pass inspection,

shrouded in a tattered bed sheet ripped in half,
tucked and clinched with safety pins. He didn't

even award me a war medal. His barber, Renzo,
had gifted my father his old, manual, wing-handled

clippers that he plowed, snicking, through my hair.
He gripped my cantaloupe of a head with his other

hand, threatened to slice off my ears if I dared
to whine or squirm. He plied a stiff pocket brush

to whisk the clippers clean, while hair snips
nettled down the back of my neck. He dribbled

a few clear beads of baby oil to lubricate
the rat-teeth of their tiny blades. In the mirror

my bald head pegged me as a young Uncle Fester,
a grinning maggot-head, a convict-in-training.

Education

A great professor, my father.
He tied my hands behind my back,

blindfolded me, taped my mouth
shut, locked me in a closet.

The darkness vast and sublime
as the night sky. He taught me

to listen to mice scratching
their wisdom behind the wall.

Pickles and Herring

Our father pickled his own half sours
and dills; brined herring he'd snagged

in fish markets, hacking off their heads,
gutting and anointing them with Kosher salt,

vinegar and spices. When he couldn't
stomach the squabbling of his two sons,

their non-stop circus, he packed each of them
into child-sized casks, not too tightly,

to let them slosh but not somersault in brine.
He'd temper them, tenderize them, season them

more to his taste. He foot-rolled each cask
across the kitchen floor into the pantry,

stood them up to cure next to his row of
ceramic crocks, plated himself some pickles

and herring, settled into his favorite chair
to bask in the brine of silence.

A Polish Summer

Hitler and Stalin spent a Polish summer
in our tenement flat in Boston's West End.
Father wanted company when

Mom cleaned downtown offices at night,
saddled him with Jurek and me.
That was when troops were still hunting them,

when Hitler, a teetotaler, began drinking.
Father shaved off their moustaches,
gave them weekly buzz cuts in the kitchen.

They looked like camp inmates.
They couldn't go barhopping,
so Father brought beer and vodka to our bunker

every day after work. Mother left
the pungent smell of *kapusta,*
of fried *cebula* and *kielbasa* on the stove.

They played poker and drank all night.
They knew a whole graveyard of jokes and told
hilarious stories about their years in power.

They pissed all their little secrets
on everyone's corpse. Each night at eight
they turned on the Polka Hour and danced,

slapping their thighs to the music,
Father joining Adolf and Jozef in whirling
around the kitchen. Sometimes the neighbors,

like the Gestapo, banged on our door.
Stalin tried to play with Jurek and me,
but he was hopeless with children.

I sat on his lap and pulled on his nose.
His breath stank. I thought he'd drink me in one gulp.
Hitler was sad we didn't have a dog so he called

Jurek and me, Bone and Fetch. They tried
to learn English by reading matchbook covers.
They unfolded old maps on the kitchen table,

re-strategized all their battles until
they erupted into fist fights. They always left
a mess for Mother while they snored,

sleeping off hangovers. She boiled and boiled
until she burst like an overcooked knockwurst.
Mom broomsticked Father in the kitchen.

It took time, but he bribed the Steczynskis
to take Hitler and Stalin off his hands.
Our lives slowly sludged back to routine.

When Father plugged candlestick lights
in the windows for Christmas, I asked him
about the time Hitler and Stalin lived with us.

It never happened, he said. *You must've dreamed it.
Or you're just stupid.* No arguing with him,
so I let it go. But I remembered vividly

how Father had loved his playtime
with Adolf and Jozef, how busy and happy he'd been;
how he loved drinking and dancing with

his buddies so much that this *kapo* of a father
forgot to whip Jurek and me with his belt
during that long, marvelous Polish Summer.

New Testament

Like Jesus, my father performed
His Father's sacred work—

whipping money lenders,
chasing them out of the temple.

But our West End tenement flat
wasn't a temple.

My brother and I
weren't money lenders.

Eviction

We weren't old enough to sit in the courtroom
with our parents. A guard in navy blue uniform,

brass buttoned, corralled me and my brother
into a waiting room, handed us coloring books,

a small cardboard box rattling with crayon stubs.
Someone had already doodled green and brown

scribbles in my book. Another page sported red
and orange streaks zagging outside the lines

in a bowl of sloppy fruit, what Miss Shapiro
in kindergarten was teaching us not to do.

I turned pages to a clean sheet—a suburban
ranch house, yard with running dog, trees and

shrubs, flower garden, a lawn for playing catch.
Nothing like our Beacon Hill brick tenement

where we played indoors when our father wasn't
home—bouncing rubber balls, trampolining

a sagging sofa, reclining on our parents' bed
and stomping the headboard, a herd of bison

thundering across the prairie until old Pani
Balczezak downstairs broomsticked her ceiling.

We weren't allowed to play on our sloping street
where every ball rolled downhill into traffic.

We had to wait for weekends when our mother,
toting a picnic bag, trekked us past Charles Station

onto the pedestrian bridge crossing Storrow Drive
to the esplanade where she unleashed us on

the great lawn fronting the Hatch Shell's giant
deaf ear. My brother and I, a snicker of monkeys,

dervished into chaos until we collapsed
beside our mother on a blanket of cool grass.

Waiting for our parents to finish in court,
I crayoned the house and yard, filling in colors,

straining to stay within the lines. The guard in
proper navy blue helped me rip the page from

the coloring book. After dinner, with Mom gone
to her cleaning job, our father announced we'd

be moving next month. I cheered and unfolded
the sheet I'd crayoned to show him where we

could live. He jerked up from the table, knocking
his chair to the floor, bursting with Polish swears.

With his clenched fist he whipped off his belt,
swinging it to color outside the lines.

Songbird

Next to our first TV
                 with its Cyclops' eye
staring from a mahogany box taller than me
perched the new canary
                    inside a chrome-plated cage,
my father's dream bird,
a two-forty-nine Woolworth special.
He promised me a stream of gold would gush
like a fountain
            from its throat.

For a week he stood before the cage whispering,
"My golden sweetie,"
                 waving his arms like a maestro,
tilting his head to profile his beak-like nose.
Neither birdseed, nor love,
              nor threats
could lead that bird into song.

It was a long, clamorous, crashing racket
before the subway
                spit us out at Savin Hill.
We'd come to Pan Krulinski,
                   the Polish Birdman,
whose canaries leaked song continuously
like broken faucets.
              Pan Krulinski lifted
an executioner's black hood off a cage
                         and whistled.
The canary burst into
              a sun shower
of warbles and trills that left my father gripping
an empty shot glass,
             leaning forward off the sofa.

Pan Krulinski prescribed exclusive birdseed,

a sunny window roost,
                        perhaps a mate.
From a squat, black, bow-front cabinet
he pulled out a 78
                        that he balanced on
a phonograph spindle—
                        it plopped down
like an egg cracked into a frying pan.
Through a forest thick with scratchy hissing
a canary sang so melodiously,
                        so deftly,
that both men closed their eyes
and nodded slowly
                        over their vodka.

Hearing that record each night for two weeks
I'd worked myself up
                        and couldn't sleep.
Perched on the rolled arm of the sofa
I reached inside
                        my father's plaid flannel shirt
draped over the cage
                        for that thing
fluttering inside those thin chrome ribs.
Even in my small palm
                        its body felt slight,
as though it could melt through my fingers,
its tiny heart
                        throbbing as fast
as a spinning 78,
                        its soft yellow body
nothing more than a tube of paste
I could squeeze dry.

My father replaced the birdcage
with a cuckoo clock.
                        Each evening,

before he turned on the TV for the local news
that he didn't understand,
he pulled the chains
                      hoisting two metal pinecones
dragging time down to the floor
so the carved wooden bird
                      couldn't fly away.

On Sundays,
          the afternoon in the apartment
trapped in an hourglass,
                  I watched TV
as my father snored on the sofa.
The wooden cuckoo mocked us
                      every hour on the hour
with its hollow, mechanical, cuckoo call;
and each hour woke my father as he
sprawled on the sofa.
                  Muttering and grumbling,
clutching a crumpled pillow to his chest,
snorting,
          coughing up his smoker's phlegm,
he shifted his weight and resettled into
a bone-rattling snoring
                  that I realized,
once I'd sat still and really listened to it,
was rhythmic,
          modulated, sonorous.
It was really quite pleasant,
                  almost musical.

My Brother's First Communion Photo

The formal family pose—
four of us standing so we don't touch.
From the back row my parents can't see
the shadows they cast against the grey backdrop

of the 20th century. They've been rounded up—
another interrogation and line-up
under glaring bright lights;
their shellshock congeals into resignation.

These World War II refugees
are cardboard cutouts in America;
eyes vacant, lips pursed, faces grim—
immigrant Gothic.

My father's slick hair fits him like a shrunken
skullcap. The wide lapels of his grey suit flare like
the tailfins of a '56 Chevy Bel Air
he never learned to drive.

He's sober now, but later today
he'll be drunk, snoring, sprawled across the sofa
as though assassinated yet again.
He's not that far removed from

his petty tyrant father's farm outside Warsaw
so abused by poverty
that his three years in a Nazi labor camp
seemed a step up.

My mother wears a navy blue dress with
an umbilical cord of fake pearls
noosed around her neck.
She still can't believe that when she

was twelve her parents banished her to
a maid's misery in a distant town,
then how the Nazis, at gunpoint, trucked her
to a labor camp in Germany,

so she clutches the coffin of her black handbag
with its wadded tissues and
the lifeline of a rosary as though someone
will snatch it from her any second.

Jurek looks tentative in his little white suit
as if this first communion business
isn't such a good idea,
but this German-born soldier of God stands guard

armed with the grenade of a prayer book
rosary-strapped to his hand
and wielding a candle like a bayonet,
shielding our father—but from what?

He doesn't know he has rheumatic fever,
that he would've died if he wasn't
rushed to the hospital the next day,
pumped full of penicillin.

I'm the all-Polish-American boy—
moon-faced, chubby-cheeked, double-chinned,
with a broad puckish grin.
An overweight child is a status symbol in Poland

so my parents encourage me to eat,
but I still can't fill out
Jurek's hand-me-down, straitjacket suit coat
hanging nearly to my knees.

With my left arm lost in the sleeve
I could be a midget war vet amputee released
from Ward 8 for the afternoon.
My brother's pants are so big on me

I've had to hoist the waist up to my chest
where it chafes my armpits.
If only I had a hidden button
I'd twirl my bowtie like a propeller.

I'm almost six years old. My parents tell me
I haven't yet reached the age of reason,
haven't tasted history or God, which could be why
I'm the only one of us smiling.

Durak

Father taught us his favorite card game,
Durak (You Fool!), from his Nazi labor camp,

the final game after playing poker for cigarettes.
He dealt five cards to himself, to Jurek, to me;

said it worked best with five or six men.
Highest card won each round. No trumps.

You followed suit. Low cards were golden.
There were no winners, only a loser.

You escaped losing when you played out
all your cards, were left empty-handed.

If you won a round, you added the cards
to those fanned in your hand.

Last man holding a spray of cards was loser.
They poured water into his shoes.

If they had to chase him through the barrack,
or outside, they pissed into his shoes.

Next day the loser worked in shoes
sopping wet, even in freezing weather.

My brother and I exchanged a sharp look
as our father laughed and laughed.

His Lost Polish Son

A child in Poland, my father
hatched a village from bones scratched

from his father's scabby farm.
He peopled it with egg shells and acorns.

Stood a bent fork in the dirt as a chapel
in whose garden he buried his mother.

Then pounded his village with a rock.
He survived 3 years in a Nazi labor camp.

Interned 5 years in a D.P. camp after the war,
he learned how to ride a bicycle.

In America he wanted me baptized *Jan,*
but the Polish priest insisted on John.

My father bought his lost Polish son toys
he'd never had—wooden alphabet blocks in

bright colors, Lincoln logs to build a home,
a spinning top that tornadoed across

all 50 states of our linoleum floor tiles.
My father taught me to ride a bicycle at 7,

then poured my first shot of vodka
I spit into the sink. He told me I was Polish.

No, I said, *I was born in America,
speak American to my friends in school.*

At home I slogged through the swamp
of speaking Polish to my father;

he never learned to walk barefoot
across burning coals to speak English.

Soup

I was seven,
            food finicky,
refused to eat my mother's cabbage soup.

It was torture—
            slimy, a sickly pale green;
a thick witch's brew with shards of pork fat
fried with flour,
            bubbling with diced potato,
anchored in a black pot with a ham bone;
topped off in a bowl
            with slices of dill pickles.

It smelt of low tide,
            of things old and sour
she should've thrown out but couldn't
because she'd survived those years
            in a Nazi labor camp
lucky to eat potato peel soup
            clear as water.

She once slapped my hand for tossing
stale bread to the floor.
            She picked it up,
brushed it off against her apron,
            blessed herself,
priested it into her mouth.

Why eat stale bread?
            I asked.
She'd just banished a warm loaf of rye
to the tin bread box doghouse
            atop the fridge.
The Nazis lost the war.
            We live in America.

She menaced her finger's metronome at me—
Food is sacred.
              Don't ever   throw it   away.

When she left to clean offices downtown
my father summoned me
                    to the kitchen table,
pointed to a chair.
                        He announced he'd had it with me.
He had so little food
                  in his labor camp
that if someone had boiled a shoe
he would've eaten it gladly,
                      would've savored
every drop of its broth.
                      I wanted to give him
the sneakers off my feet,
                but kept silent.

He ladled me a bowl
                  of my mother's soup,
unsheathed his belt,
                doubled it in his fist.
He stood above me tall as the Statue of Liberty,
ordered me to eat,
                belt twitching in his clenched fist.

I lowered my eyes,
            sat quietly as a gravestone,
folded my hands in my lap
                  as though saying grace.
I refused to touch the spoon,
                refused to eat
from the same plate
              history had served my father.

Before he began whipping me,
                         he swore at me,
quivering with rage,
                 certain I was one of the boys
who'd tossed him into the pond
                         when he couldn't swim.

As if he could teach me history
                       to keep himself alive.
As if he could lead us both
                into the Promised Land.
As if his belt were a lifeline
                   to save himself, a boy
still drowning
            in a scummy pond's awful soup.

As if.

Exquisite

What was my father thinking when he scattered
rice on the kitchen floor? Planting seeds on his

father's farm? Preaching a parable? Or was he
an archangel gifting virtue, justice, and light

to the world? He ordered me to roll my pant legs
above my knees. To kneel on the rice.

With the noose of his doubled belt hanging
from his fist, I had no choice, just as he didn't

when the *kapo* gave him orders. The rice kernels
spiked their knife points into my knees, bucked

against the bone of my knee caps. I nearly fainted.
The pain excruciating. Exquisite. Years later

I recognized myself in Bernini's Ecstasy of
St. Theresa. The grimace of her little death

lifting me outside of my body to witness a father
beating his son with a belt while the boy knelt

in fire. As if the father had scripted a new station
of the cross. After he raged out of the kitchen,

I slid onto my side to catch my breath, then
wedged a butter knife's tip to gouge out each

rice kernel emblooded in my knees. My father
commanded me to sweep the rice kernels,

rinse them in a sieve, dry them on a dish towel
to be saved in a blue cup for tomorrow's dinner.

THREE

Ritual

When he finished with me
my father put his belt back on.

I hugged him until
he stopped crying,

then guided him back to his room
down the darkened hallway,

tucked him into his bed
of broken glass.

Gifts

My father fixed my broken chair
with a single shot of vodka,

built a bicycle from cigarette butts,
a couch from shattered bricks.

He sewed teddy bears from snow,
cobbled shoes from chicken soup,

tailored dust and hair into sweaters,
trained my socks to trill like canaries.

He planted bent, rusty nails
that grew into succulent tomatoes,

taught his shoes to cook dinner
while he poured me a glass of smoke.

As he lay dying, he promised
he'd turn his corpse into my bed.

Sweet Nothings

Swaying before our apartment door, our father
fumbled his keys. His two sons had pestered him
all evening, buzzing his ears to leave Zubrycki's

all-day party where he'd sat enthroned at a table
whose skyline of booze bottles upstaged his view of
postwar Manhattan from his immigrant ship.

A barnyard odor hooked the nose of this Polish peasant
trapped in the wrong country, the wrong century,
reeled him into the pantry where my cat Kiki,

locked indoor all Sunday, his litter box chock full,
had dropped some sweet nothings into one of
my father's church shoes. He slammed shut

both kitchen doors, cursed the cat slinking beneath
a chair, skimmed off his belt in one practiced,
buccaneer swoosh, doubled it in his fist.

A scrunched-up ball of black fur scooted under
the table, its yellow eyes huge, bulging like blisters.
My father—swearing, clutching the table's edge,

beating the cat whose yowling warped the air.
The belt's thwacks were gunshots in the kitchen.
He knocked over a chair, shoved me aside.

Kiki dashed past the sink, howled behind the stove.
I screamed for my father to stop, not to kill my cat.
He was in such a rage I thought he'd kill me next,

then rush back to Poland to kill, yet again, his
already dead father for often beating him like this.
Kiki hurled himself against a locked door,

bounced off to scurry around the kitchen, its red
linoleum floor on fire. He kept yowling and bounding
around the kitchen. My father kept chasing

and beating him, determined to cure him forever
of being a cat. I unlatched the back door and Kiki
bolted, blurring down the stairs into the cellar.

My father tossed his belt onto the kitchen table
knocking over the salt and pepper shakers.
He opened the fridge, poured himself a glass of milk.

Satan

Our father brought Satan home from
the Polish-American Citizens Club. Scared shitless by
his alligator skin, the horns on his forehead,
oily smoke rising from his skull,
my brother and I hid, shivering, under our beds.

But Satan turned out to be one hell of a guy—
a whiz with household chores
who vacuumed a room in under a minute,
a marvel in the kitchen, a virtuoso of victuals
commanding exotic spices into celestial harmonies,

unlike our mother who boiled vegetables into
a swamp. Satan sailed through
the sink's stack of dirty dishes, skimmed through yard work
and house repairs, then danced the mazurka,
our father whistling and stomping his feet.

Satan burst out laughing at our father's crude, filthy jokes,
lit our father's cigarettes with a flaming fingertip
while they knocked back vodka shots.
Then, snacking on popcorn, his cloven hooves
propped on a sagging hassock, Satan chuckled at

the cartoons my brother and I watched on TV.
I lay in the bathtub when Satan took a piss,
glimpsed two tiny horns tipping the head of his penis.
He attended Sunday Mass with us, convinced
our father to kneel in the front pew. At the altar rail

Father Stanislaw beamed as he jeweled a communion wafer
onto Satan's forked, quivering tongue.
Satan was the father our father had never had, the son
he'd always wanted. My brother and I
prayed each night that Satan would never leave.

Lucky

After putting his belt back on
my father said
              I was lucky—

His father beat him
with a leather shaving strop.
He'd had to wipe off his own blood
and, a week later,
              peel strips of dead skin
off his arms and shoulders.

How he could never quite reach
the dead skin on his back.

Handyman

        I

Our father was industrious, inventive—
he managed home repairs and improvements
with castoffs salvaged from
neighbors' trash.

The hammer handle he whittled, sanded,
and screwed onto a spatula head
after its hand-grip broke.

The kitchen cabinet minus doors
he lugged home to be reborn a television stand
with storage space below
that he wallpapered the same as the living room.

The tin can he flattened, trimmed, crimped into
a tiny dustpan, then screwed to a stub of broom stick;
an old paint brush to sweep up dirt
collecting in window wells.

        II

Jurek and I, 9 and 7, watched
our father set to work in the evening kitchen
on the wooden shaft of a toilet plunger
whose rubber dome had split.

He sawed 14 inches from the shaft,
then snipped 18 inches from an old leather belt.

With yardstick and ballpoint pen
he measured and marked the leather band
length-wise into 6 thin strips.

With metal-cutting shears he carefully, methodically—
his tongue bulging out a cheek—
slit 6 thongs 14 inches long.
He folded 4 inches of unslit leather belt

over the pole's stump,
nailed brads to both sides,
trussed it with reclaimed fishing line.

My brother and I
                shared a glance.
Without spilling a single word we stood up
from our chairs, muffled toward our bedroom,
quietly clicked the door closed.

        III

A *kapo* in our father's labor camp
must've had a scourge like this.

When our mother worked at night
our father lashed us with it—
those leather thongs slithering and stinging
like Medusa's snaky hair.

He said one taste of it would teach us more
than a belt ever could.

        IV

He kept the scourge on his bureau.
After he used it, he'd grip it like
a riding crop, slapping it against his thigh
as if strutting in jackboots.

Before bed my brother and I
compared our welts—
who'd received the biggest one?

Father struggled to smelt, refine us into perfect boys,
but we couldn't stop squabbling
over toys or cookies, or stop
throwing pillows, scuffling, shrieking.

Then he'd appear, like a burning bush,
blocking the doorway,
twitching his whip.

If only he'd devised a way to wire our fear
he could've lit
all 6 houses on our block.

    V

A few months later it hit me at
my first communion bash.
My parents' Polish friends were there—survivors, all,
of Nazi labor camps.

While adults boozed in the kitchen,
lions lounging in tall grass around a watering hole,
their children burrowed through our apartment
past a dead Christ crucified in every room.

In no time they discovered my father's scourge
and knew exactly what it was because
their parents beat them with canes, strops, or belts.
But even they were stunned.

One kid said, "He beats you with *this*?"

    VI

I knew our father had gone too far.
I hatched a scheme—
to hell with consequences.

I wheedled my brother into conspiracy.
We'd saddle the half hour between
our mother's departure for work at four,
our father's arrival at four-thirty,
then race full-tilt forward.

It seemed futility equal to
the Polish cavalry's charge, swords drawn,
against German Panzers.

While Jurek clamped the scourge
over the kitchen table's edge,
I sawed the handle into one-inch nuggets
that dropped, like petrified turds, onto the floor.

We took turns with the shears to snip
all 6 leather thongs into bits
that even our father couldn't salvage.

My brother swept up the sawdust.
I dumped the wood and leather scraps into a pile on
our father's bureau. A deliberate defecation
before the statue of the Blessed Virgin Mother
who stood serenely in a sky blue mantle,
arms open wide to the world,
her bare foot crushing the devil serpent's head.

VII

Our father was stunned by what we'd done.
He kept staring, speechless,
at his scourge transfigured into trash,
a pile of junk on his bureau.

Then a hint of a smile passed his lips as if,
hard to believe, his sons could be
so industrious, inventive.

Kiki

My cat came home wild,
foaming at the mouth.

Wearing thick leather gloves,
my father caught Kiki

in a cellar corner,
grabbed his hatchet.

I watched as he
settled the matter.

Dancing with My Father

I

Sweet summer evening.
As I played with friends on our street

my father rushed at me,
clutched my right hand in his left hand

to yank me home.
I skipped and jumped to keep up with him

as he whipped me with a belt
looped in his right fist.

I was yelping and dancing—
part polka, part mazurka—

to the music of my father's belt
slicing the summer air.

II

In late June 1942 German soldiers
danced with my father on his farm

in God's country before transporting him
to a Nazi labor camp in Germany

for the duration of the war,
or however long he might survive.

Strongman

I leaned back against the wall, my brother
sloshing in the bathtub. Stretching my arms

above my shoulders, then behind me,
I lifted the reverse barbell of the towel bar,

powered my pretzel pose until I wrenched it
from the wall. I thought the bathtub

with my brother sailing in it had dropped
onto my back. Father rushed to see

my latest stunt. Another belt beating?
He hoisted me into his arms, lowered me

onto his bed, rubbing my back, dusting off
his prize turnip. When I could sit up

without wincing, he opened the warehouse
of his Slavic slurs, smacked my head.

I closed my eyes to hear the ringing in my ears.
If I jumped off the roof, would he catch me?

If I bolted through speeding traffic, would he
lead me to safety? If I was drowning, would he

toss me one end of his belt to reel me back
to shore? Who was the real strongman here?

How had he swum the full length of the war,
then walked across the ocean to America?

The Connoisseur of Cow Manure

(for Judy Delogu)

Each spring the hardware store stocked garden supplies.
My father displayed the label he'd scissored from his

depleted bag of Bovung Brand Dehydrated Cow Manure—
featuring the picture of a cow—because he knew

only Polish, not English. He slung the 20-lb bag over
his shoulder, lugged it home through crowds and traffic,

irked he had to pay for cow manure in America.
Before setting his many seeds and seedlings,

he laid an under bed of loam manure-mixed to his
exacting standards, careful to use just enough manure

to not scorch the whisper of roots. That first year
I invaded one of his seeded rows, troweled a trench

to bury my dead plastic soldiers. He smacked my head,
smudging it with cow manure to help my hair grow.

He measured fistfuls of manure into a bucket of water,
brewing his dark tea for spot ladling, the manure

steeping to a rich, earthy, pungent smell. All summer
he baptized his garden with his kitchen ladle,

blessing his tomatoes, cucumbers, beans, and peas.
When nature called he ducked behind the back stairs

to piss into his bucket of manure tea to pack it
with extra punch. What he'd always done in Poland.

Something

Maybe I did something,
or maybe I *didn't* do
something, but my father
unsheathes his belt, doubles it
in his fist, starts beating me,
teaching me how the world
works, proving that fathers
can eat their own children.
But when I'm not food enough
he starts beating the sofa,
the framed family photos,
the dead man nailed to a wall.
It's as if every promise
his father made was a lie,
honey smeared in his eyes
to blind him, so he stumbles
outside beating parked
cars, beating houses
with boarded windows,
beating brick walls, beating
a leaning telephone pole,
beating the STOP sign
at street's end, beating
the corner store where he
buys cigarettes and vodka,
until he drops to sit on
the granite curb, his belt
exhausted and panting
beside him. I'm only eight
but I know what to do—
I run to him, drape my
small arm around his
shoulder, help him stand
up, thread his belt back
through his pant loops.
I hold his hand. He's my
father. I lead him home.

Intimacy

I studied
my father's face

when fury
ripped off his leash

and he belt-whipped me.
His face burning,

contorting.
Eyes startled open.

Teeth clenched behind
grimacing lips.

Panting.
Grunting.

Like a dog
banging a bitch.

Father's Day

Our father woke us with a furious commotion
in the kitchen; he'd fractured himself into

three tiny fathers, naked, each one two-feet tall.
They blamed each other for their predicament.

A fist fight and wrestling match ensued. Each
claimed he was Tadek. These three dads were

our holy trinity—husband, father, drunk.
They were fierce and nasty, three razor blades

of rivalry and rage. My mother diapered all
three snarling, savage brats in dish towels.

They were a litter of lion cubs, I said; let's keep
the tamest one, place two others with families

who need an angry, teeny-weeny father.
Mother shouted, NO. They were her pint-sized

darlings—Ted, Tad, and Todd. She'd raise them
as her own children. Enroll them in grammar

school. They could learn a soupcon of French,
a slice of algebra, and, finally, to read and write

English. One last chance to become American.
But first we had to buy them childrens clothes

that fit, purchase a whole party of toys, stock
the pantry with miniature shot bottles of vodka.

Friday Nights

If my father wasn't home by nine-thirty when
my mother returned from work, she flared

into panic, like those nights when drunken
German guards invaded the hen house of

her labor camp barrack. Twenty years later,
she's still root-bound with terror. Had Tadek

been robbed? beaten? arrested? even worse?
Such a relief, an hour later, when he staggered

up the slow stairs singing off-key a ditty he'd
carried from Poland. Once he'd settled into

his kitchen chair, she resurrected her anger
about his drinking, pissing away their money,

his failure to stand a better husband, father.
He understood why she erupted like this, why

she turned so frantic, but why couldn't she
relinquish her daily dread of impending disaster?

They were no longer in Germany! He blustered,
raved, stood up and threw his glass of milk

against a kitchen wall, but never raised his
calloused hands to her. He exhausted himself

at work, he said, needed to bust loose weekends.
He'd been born with vodka in his blood, refused

to deny his birthright. I hid in the hall behind
a door, so petrified by their bickering that

they hog-tied me in their labor camp bunk,
while Jurek turned the TV's volume louder

to drown out the kitchen drama. Is this how
marriage worked? Head-butting grievances?

All arguments sharpened into knives?
They still quarreled about that dead milkhorse

they'd buried in the kitchen. I steeled myself
to slit the Easter lamb's throat, to smear its

hot blood on my parents' foreheads to dupe
the angel of death living in our house.

Winter Father

When the blizzard and deep freeze hit
Friday night, our father didn't return
from Dudek's bar. The next morning, shoveling,

Jurek and I found his body in front of our house.
He'd almost made it home!
A shame to waste a perfectly good frozen corpse,

so we grabbed rope, the kitchen's sharpest knife.
We sliced off our father's clothes—
so much easier to drag him over snow and ice,

to haul him up the long hill in the park.
Jurek, reading Greek myths in school, called us
Brothers Sisyphus. At the summit,

exhausted, we found a swarm of Polish kids,
bundled up, Bruegheled into sledding their dead,
naked, frozen fathers down the hill.

If only our father could witness this delight.
Off to the side, someone had already
devised a pulley system of ropes rigging

tree trunks to hoist our fathers uphill.
Jurek and I took a running start
and launched our father downhill.

We mounted his corpse in tandem,
me in front, Jurek in back steering with
our father's frozen penis.

FOUR

Brief World

I blew a solar system of soap bubbles
from a third-floor window,
                                and my father,
tending his hard green tomatoes,
                                   glanced up.

I waved to him,
                 but all he saw
were dark wet bruises
                         where soap bubbles had burst
on grey clapboards.
                    He swore at me,
rushed upstairs,
               belt already doubled in his fist.

Who could explain to this man
                         who'd never blown soap bubbles
on his scar of a farm in Poland?
                             How they grazed in space?
The grace of their quivering fragility?
                                Their translucence
that delighted us,
                  or distorted our view?
Those slick rainbows
                    of continents and oceans
swirling on their skin?
                     Their dreamy existence before
the wind's laughter popped them
                          against our house?

Who could tell us that we were trapped
inside a soap bubble
                   drifting blindly,
lost in sunlight?
             The tension of anger between us
what kept our brief world afloat.

Birdcalls

To comfort himself my father sounded piercing,
screeching birdcalls. A murder of crows

prompted him everywhere, flocking him like
a black cloak cawing and squawking. A jury

of vultures presided on our flat roof's ledge.
The apartment swelled with starlings, a serpentine

swarm swirling in every room. You couldn't walk
down the hall, arms over your head, without being

pecked and bloodied. At all the windows countless
birds bashed their beaks at the glass to bust outside,

while my father watched TV, his oily black wings
folded tightly to fit into his easy chair.

Bruised Light

My father roamed the labyrinth inside his body
with its dead ends and lost alleys.

Each morning he rose from sleep
and clothed himself in flames.

All that bruised light he nailed to his walls.

He lived in a house that was always burning.

Each match he struck flickered into a bird
that flew away.

At night he found comfort in walking on
the river paved with darkness.

He never realized he was pure light
when he burned.

Father's Garden

White peonies and lush red roses raise
the Polish flag in his garden. The yellow iris

and orange daylilies are pastries his mother
baked. He shells, eats sweet peas the moment

he snaps a bulging pod. Those stubby cukes
tucked under nursery mounds of cooling leaves

will crunch in his salad, or bask in quart jars
with spices, dill, salt, vinegar. His green tomatoes

long for August heat to Rubens their bellies
red, sweet, and succulent. This summer air so

fragrant and soothing, he can almost forget
the hard-packed soil in his German labor camp

grew only weeds stringy and prickly, but not
impossible to chew into a mash and swallow.

Ode to a Sofa

                I

Even as a smartass sophomore at BC High
in madras sports coat and wide green paisley tie,

I couldn't believe how ugly, how uncomfortable
it was—the sofa my father dragged upstairs

off the street. Boxy, curbstone low to the ground,
propped on conical V-legs, its thin cushions

hard as lumber, upholstered in steel wool.
This was an ascetic's dream hair-shirt sofa,

like one of the many punishments
my father endured in a Nazi labor camp.

Now shorter than me, he retreated into
the kitchen. His fingers fiddled with the salt

and pepper shakers. In Poland, he said,
we never even had a sofa. He wouldn't make

eye contact. **You** wanted a Catholic High School—
That costs money! He suffered my silence

as long as he could. **Son of a bitch! It's a sofa!
In a few years we'll toss it into the trash!**

                II

It's all my father knew—the wobbly chairs,
the old tools and broken gadgets he rescued from

the neighbors' trash. Those drunken Friday nights
at the Polish Club. The Masses in Latin

he withstood against the back wall of the church
behind 10 empty pews. The 2-week vacations

he worked through to earn double-time pay.
The car he never bought or learned to drive.

His one suit, a grey, double-breasted beauty
with baggy pants that cast him in 50's

gangster movies well into the Age of Aquarius.
The wedge of rye bread he used to wipe

the last bacon drippings in the frying pan.
That pickle jar of found coins it took him

18 years to fill. The scrap metal he scavenged
and sold for 16 cents per pound.

His obsequious tone with anyone in uniform
or seated behind a desk. The heart attack

that killed him 20 years later when this sofa
was still parked in the living room.

A Lifetime

My father boxcut cardboard into squares
he tied into bundles, stockpiled on the sidewalk.

A tidy stack for the garbage men. So efficient,
so considerate. In his labor camp he didn't want

to trench the corpses, then cover them beneath
shovelfuls of dirt, or pour gasoline to set them

blazing. He would've preferred wrapping them
with canvas, tying each one with rope braided in

the underground factory where his wife-to-be
was prisoner. He'd lay the dead men head-to-toe,

precisely, and prop another course of corpses
on top of the first row as if building a wall, or

foundation for a house, piling bodies like a boy
stacking wooden blocks—slowly constructing

a pyramid with all the corpses he'd ever handled,
toiling a lifetime to build his monument.

His Last Job

I

He was midnight's servant in the overnight
two-man crew who soaked, scrubbed, scoured

all the surfaces inside the meat-packing plant.
The work as difficult, dirty, and draining as

anything he'd done in his Nazi labor camp.
Now in his grey-hair sixties he worked 8 hours

a day, 5 days each week, instead of staggering
2 weeks of 12-hour days with one day off.

This job offered him a paycheck, a 2-week
vacation, paid insurance, for Christmas—a ham.

II

In heavy rubber gloves and boots, he wrestled
with the grease of animals anointing every inch

of those meat rooms, those slick cement floors
sloped to center drains, the slippery filth stamped

all over the bathroom. He sprayed pressurized
hot-water hoses; handled industrial cleansers—

congesting his breathing, triggering stinging tears—
to scrub the ubiquitous grease, to kill the stench

of meat in the steamfog trapped by windows
nailed shut and fortified with iron bars.

III

He scored steel wool to scour the grudge of grease
from steel work tables and stainless steel vats

big enough to boil missionaries; butcher knives,
cleavers, bone saws, electric saw blades, meat hooks

that, in daytime, dangled carcasses from which
butchers cut slabs and trimmed strips of flesh

they tossed into the vats, then married with brine
and spices that the inverted devil's scepters

of blades spiked on metal stems pulverized
into a pinkish-grey slop to be extruded into

bulging pork-gut casings which they looped
and coiled next to the black flanks of pastrami

suspended like bombs on steel rolling racks they
wheeled—squealing—into the smoke room oven.

IV

Those racks—the worst part of the job. Encrusted
with baked-on, blackened grease to be chiseled

and scraped each night so, in the morning,
the process would begin again, leaving my father

drained, exhausted, drenched in sweat.
Each night changing into dry clothes three times

only to be drenched again in 30 minutes,
his skin still slimed by the sludge of animal fat.

He never felt clean. For protection from thugs,
the boss locked his crew inside the plant

without any keys. A certain death trap in a fire.
He worked because he'd always had to work.

He'd work until he dropped dead on the job,
and they paraded his carcass in the street.

The Past

Before dancing started at George's wedding,
after the Polish anthem had proclaimed that

Poland Hasn't Yet Disappeared, we ate slabs
of meat wounded and traumatized. I considered

asking my father why he'd cooked his sons with
his belt so hard, so often when we were kids.

This wasn't the right time or place. My father
clutched his highball with the same authority

he'd gripped his belt. Hundreds of years of
Polish history had herded us to feed together

at this family trough. All the horrors this
peasant king had endured had framed him,

so he yoked both his American sons to haul
a train of wagons loaded with history's sludge.

But, haul it where? Did he expect us to spread
this manure over all the fields we passed?

Stretching into the horizon in all directions
as far as our father could see, the future was

disguised as the distant past. All around us farms
raged with endless crops, their roots gripping

the soil with no apology, clutching at whatever
they could feed on, determined never to let go.

(Footnote: Lines 2 & 3 reference the Polish national anthem, *Poland Hasn't Yet Disappeared* (or *Poland Is Not yet Lost*). Poland was often at the mercy of its stronger neighbors. From 1795 to 1918 Poland had been partitioned by Germany, Russia, the Austrian-Hungarian Empire and didn't exist as a country. After the Treaty of Versailles created Poland again in 1918, it existed as a country for 21 years until it was partitioned once more by Germany and

Russia at the start of World War II. The lyrics for a Polish folk tune, that later became the national anthem, were written 1797. It wasn't until 1926 that *Poland Hasn't Yet Disappeared* became the official Polish national anthem.)

Pijewski & Sons

After I bought my first triple decker I subscribed to
my brother's business model from Amos Tuck—

leverage assets, borrow against growing equity
to plow back into more real estate. The rising tide

of home values was now floating all mortgages.
My father pissed on my plans. He shunned risk like

a vampire recoiling from a crucifix. I glow-balled it,
defined rental property as chickens on a farm

producing ever more broods of hens roosting
on their nest eggs. Once they hatched and matured

they could be baked, roasted, stewed, fried, or bbq-ed.
Self-perpetuating dinners that'll feed us for a lifetime.

But my father was still reluctant, until I showed him
the balance sheet for the newest house in my stable.

He strolled the grassy riverbank of the cash flow
from three Cambridge rents, marveled like a tourist

at these extravagant views. Then he was happy to take
the subway's senior discount when my brother and I

were handcuffed to the office. He had keys to all
apartments in his black-leather tool bag, a doctor

making house calls, ready to brave small repairs,
to welcome the plumber or electrician, to sign for

appliance deliveries. His new dream job. He felt
useful, needed, an essential cog in the enterprise,

the utility guy we penciled in behind the plate or
at second base. But he came loaded with baggage.

Convinced he knew more than we did, he always
offered unasked-for advice, liked to lord orders,

a grizzly bear dressed as flannel-shirted foreman.
He thought he governed the family organization,

il capo, managing his sons with calm and sage
counsel so we wouldn't screw it up. A small price

to pay for all parties in Pijewski & Sons to harvest
the hay, but still manage to roll in it. For once

it felt like a genuine family. I could breathe easier,
treasure the lack of acrimony, bask in the partnership

of father and sons plowing that fertile black soil of
the family's back forty. This was our golden age.

1001 Polish Nights

My father had thought withholding his stories
would keep him alive, but if he'd been drinking

when I visited, he answered questions he'd refused
to answer before. I visited him each week to drink

in his kitchen. Drink by drink his stories dribbled
out, leaking into the cellar beneath the door

he'd crucified shut. Those early wounds—
the sledge hammer of a father, poverty married to

his mother's corpse, his first wife and daughter dead.
All that weight he'd hauled in a labor camp—

the exhaustion, boredom, and hopelessness;
the constant hunger and threat of violence;

the unimaginable stench; men who'd burrowed
into their graves for safety; the stories they told and

retold, the jokes they shared, always jokes—
the blacker, more bitter, the better. Then he clawed up

shards of what he'd buried—the ugly things men
did to survive; all those betrayals, beatings, murders;

bodies piled on bodies, gasoline flames raging
out of control; how he nearly slid down a knife's edge

into despair like some of his friends. He'd sutured
his wounds with barbed wire, but forty years later

they were still open and bleeding, blinding
his kitchen with watchtower searchlights.

Ziggy's Body

I

Vodka smudged my father's phone voice.
I always told him, if you live like a dog, you'll die

like a dog. He was talking about Zdzislaw, his son
from Poland, my half brother—Ziggy in Boston.

Monstrously drunk, Ziggy had tumbled down
the stairs in his flophouse. The police slowly

explained my father's choice—either claim
his son's body, or let the city bury him

in an unmarked pauper's grave. Ziggy, 46,
now lost to the enduring stench of history.

II

Three when his mother died giving birth;
four when he witnessed his father transported,

at gunpoint, to a Nazi labor camp in Germany.
Zdzislaw, his name meaning "warrior,"

abandoned to his grandfather, a brutal drunk.
What oozed and bubbled up in that black hole?

Citizened in 1960, my father sponsored his son
to America. Within weeks, he was eager

to return Zdzislaw to Poland as if he'd been
a rash, reckless purchase. So it continued—

a torn scroll of expectations. A boiling cauldron
of anger. Drunken threats. Kitchen knives

stashed in a closet. Police arrests. His marriage
down the drain. Two young sons abandoned.

Bouts of failed detox. Drunken visits to dad
to bum more cash. Passed out in doorways

and alleys near the Our Lady of Czestochowa
grammar school his two sons attended.

>   III

As if things couldn't get worse. Police called,
asked me to identify Zdzislaw. His skull

bashed in with a baseball bat for his cashed
welfare check. Biking to classes at BU, I stopped

at Boston City Hospital on skid row. Behind wire-
reinforced glass Ziggy lay buried in a coma,

a steel plate in his skull. His head wrapped
in white gauze—a maharaja waiting to begin

his dream life of milk, honey, and gold.
I nodded to the policeman.

>   IV

Last time I saw Zdzislaw alive—August 1983—
three months before he died. I was 31, landlord,

a budding real estate entrepreneur. On a first date
I showed Teresa the highlights of blue collar

Boston, the Polish neighborhood straddling
my home corner of Dorchester and Southie—

the crowded, wooden triple-decker tenements;
Grzesik's Market; the Polish church and school.

And there was Ziggy in the buttery summer
dusk, so drunk he couldn't stand up, sagging

against the Polish-American Citizens Club,
shoring up the yellow brick road of its façade.

I told Teresa the drunk was my half brother,
spilled some of his story. No second date.

V

I had to convince my CPA brother, George,
we should claim Ziggy's body, give him

a church service and burial. He itemized
all the damage our half brother had inflicted.

If our father could abandon Ziggy, he could
abandon us too. We knew our father had

a clenched fist for a heart. No need to let him
keep kicking Ziggy's corpse. I worked George

until he agreed. We'd split the cost and I'd do
all the phone calls, leg work, paperwork.

CPA George tallied the bottom line—
It'd be worth the money just to be rid of him.

VI

On the phone my father exploded.
How dare you** get involved in this!* ***He's not your son!

He's my brother, I said. You didn't claim his body, so I did.
But he's not your son!

I pressed him: so shameful for a father
to refuse to bury his son. He hung up on me.

An hour later, he called back. *Zdzislaw was my son.
I want to bury him. I'm claiming his body.*

You lost your chance, I said.
But I'm his father, I want to bury him. Give me his body!

I paused, spoke softly.
Ziggy's body, legally, belongs to me.

VII

We'd stumbled into our own little Trojan War,
a grotesque comedy routine by

Abbotski and Costellowicz. A father desperate for
the return of Hector's body dragged around Troy.

Priam and I deadlocked in our siege of stupidity.
I proposed we slice Zdzislaw's body in two—

we'd each get…

My long pause embraced my father's stone silence.
That's when I caved.

Last Time

Last time I saw my father he wanted to kill me.
I'd just quit the office job I hated to convert

my Cambridge triple-decker into condos. I enlisted
my handyman dad to repoint the brick foundation.

He'd demonstrate, I'd take it from there. I thought
we'd both work, two of us toiling could do twice

as much, but he had tools for himself only.
He wanted me to watch his technique, to learn

his little tricks—gouging out crumbling mortar
with a screwdriver, scruffing out the grit with

a wire brush, mixing mortar in a shallow pan,
flicking water from a wet paint brush into clefts

between bricks before pointing fresh mortar from
his hawk with a convex blade, wiping off excess

with a barely moistened sponge. I was eager to
work. This wasn't heart surgery. So in my father's

finest tradition I improvised—plywood for a
palette, butter knife as repointing tool, the back

of a teaspoon to smooth off the mortar I'd mixed
in a dented sauce pan. The old man exploded.

You're fucking it up. You need masonry tools.
I wanted to keep working, said I'd buy the tools

that night, work tomorrow, a head start before
leaving for vacation—my first in five long years.

My father glared at me, his fist squeezing the life
out of his sponge. He believed I'd fall on my face,

lose the house and all my money. I was an idiot
if I thought anyone would ever buy my condos.

Since I'd already quit my job, I'd dug myself into
a grave. He'd refuse to return to work at 70

to support his failed son. Said I had to cancel my
trip, abandon this project, beg my boss for my old

job. He was furious with me. He was going home
now, taking his tools. Said he'd ***never*** step into

my house again. I'd blundered into the noose
of my father's wartime fear of uncertainty, of risk.

When I offered him a ride home, he told me
to go to hell. Rather than go to hell, I drove to

Somerville Lumber for tools, stopped to buy film.
Days later, while I drove a white Toyota Celica

along the Pacific redwood coast, a heart attack
killed my father as he prepped his garden for

tomatoes, as if he'd staked his life to prove how
wrong I was, as if he had to have the final word.

The Wake

My brother's officemate with fiancée
arrived at the wake. The moment she saw

my father lying in the open casket wearing
his only suit—light grey, double-breasted,

newly pressed—she burst out sobbing.
As if he, too, were her father.

George's hand settled on her shoulder.
I said our father had lived a long life;

his heart attack had been quick, merciful.
But she couldn't stop sobbing.

Maybe she realized, when she saw him in
the casket, that everyone she knows will die—

her parents, siblings, all of her friends
from school, even the children to whom

she hadn't yet given birth. She'd stepped
into the spotlight as star of the show,

consigned the dapper gent in the casket with
a full head of white hair and perfect makeup

to a minor role in a 1940's B movie.
And I felt so grateful she was sobbing;

the professional mourner stealing the scene.
She didn't know my father, or anything

about him, but she was gifting him
a gorgeous, fragrant bouquet of tears

that, no matter how hard I tried,
I couldn't will myself to shed.

FIVE

Coffin

I stand over
my father's open coffin.

His corpse begins
to quiver,

eyes opening
slowly.

He turns his head
to face me,

whispers,
If I were you,

*I wouldn't
forgive me either.*

Taking Out the Trash: ONE

At night I lug two black plastic garbage bags
outside. I'm surprised to see my father standing

on the sidewalk. I haven't seen him since he died
three years ago. He says he can't sleep so he walks;

he's strolled by my house before but never stopped.
This time he'd like to step inside, maybe sit down

for a few drinks. He hasn't had one, he says, since
he died. I'm unnerved by how much rage I feel.

I drop the two garbage bags at his feet. Tell him
he's not welcome here. He says nothing. Shrugs.

Walks away. He steps slowly down the street
as though to the corner store for a quart of milk.

Son of Dracula

Nothing good on TV, so
I reach beneath the couch for my crowbar,
pry the thick oak lid off the coffee table coffin.

I tug at the wooden stake sunk deep
in my father's heart,
root it out;
grab the lapels of his high-collared black cape,
slap him awake.

When his dark eyes clear and he sees
it's me, he shudders.
I shake him until his pale, wizened head
snaps back and forth.
His tongue's pink slug squirms in his mouth.
He slobbers syllables like slime.

Please, he whispers, *leave me alone.
I'm dead.*

You bastard, I say,
you're never going to die.

He extends two twisted fingers in a feeble V.
He wants a cigarette, a shot of vodka.
When I say, *No,* he cringes
as though I've flashed him a crucifix.

I lift him up by his neck,
drag him on a house tour of all our crypts.

Already the neighbors have gathered with torchlight,
jeering, jabbing pitchforks into the night.
My father begins bawling, begging me
to let him die.

His raggedy dad body is limp in my arms.
So shriveled and frail,
he weighs no more than a homesick child.

Rocks come crashing through the windows,
torchlight shadows dancing on our stone walls.
I lower my father, sobbing quietly,
into the crib of his coffin.

I slick back his thin wispy hair,
rouge his lips with bootblack,
give his dry white neck a deep goodnight kiss,
then hammer that wooden stake home into his heart.

The neighbors are pounding on our door,
shouting for you to come out.

Don't worry, Dad.
You're safe here with me---
I'll never let them take you away.

The Brothers Pijewski

On the phone, Jurek's stern voice crackled,
launched a lightning bolt at my head.

*I hold you personally responsible for the death
of **my** father.* I forgot, instantly, why I'd called

my brother. *If you hadn't argued with him all
those years, he'd still be alive.* My silence must've

inflamed him. No wonder he slammed down
the phone. A year after we'd buried our father,

the caldera of my brother's rage still stoked
earthquakes beneath his feet. What could I say

to let him understand? How could I begrudge
our other brother, Grief, for distorting Jurek's

expectations? For igniting the anger in this new
father with an infant son? As if he imagined

I had the power to do the one thing even God
couldn't do---to save our father from himself.

Dead Father

My father's corpse is drunk again,
passed out in an alley. No matter

how many times I bury him, he always
claws himself out of his grave.

*   *   *

He blocks traffic by dragging
his coffin behind him.

I help him lug it onto a bus
for Poland and wave goodbye.

*   *   *

I have no idea what to do
with all those cases of

hand grenades and jars of pickles
he'd stockpiled in his bedroom.

*   *   *

Now he slow bakes
his leather belts for days

upon days until they're
tender and delicious.

*   *   *

I've had his corpse stuffed and
laid out as if napping on the sofa.

Each night I plug him into a device
that helps him to snore.

*   *   *

While brushing snow off my car
I notice, again and again,

that each snow flake displays
his sharp, Slavic face.

      *   *   *

Even though he's been stuffed
his corpse still branches with

enough succulent fruit
to sustain us through the winter.

      *   *   *

He climbs up a ladder to face
Christ nailed on the cross,

tilts an open pint of vodka
to Christ's eager, bleeding lips.

      *   *   *

He joy-rides his convertible coffin
up and down Beacon Street.

He pulls over to ask if I'll join him
in picking up some hot babes.

      *   *   *

His body parts keep turning up
in my closet, behind doors,

under my bed. I use them
to cook fabulous soup.

      *   *   *

Standing in St. Peter's Square
I see him, majestic,

bigger than a Zeppelin,
cruising above the Vatican.

        *   *   *

Please, his corpse says, *no kielbasa jokes.*
I didn't survive those years

in a Nazi labor camp
just to become your punch line.

Someone's Father

I strolled into a neighborhood bar on Pluto
and met my father for the first time.

We traded rounds of drinks, fell into life stories
of such unbearable heartbreak even before

he survived the boiling cauldron of a world war.
After a long pause, he ripped off convoluted,

outlandish stories that knotted me in stitches.
We began airing our too-numerous regrets;

all the little triumphs we'd accomplished,
or not. We laughed at the glorious stupidity

of our deepest, dumbest, diddly secrets;
those screw-ups we'd pay anything to re-do.

Then a round of backslaps after we downed
our final drink. He still seemed like an enigma;

the last man in the world I could imagine
as someone's father, anyone's son.

Homecoming

When my father returned after many years
he didn't recognize either of his parents,

or his two brothers digging in the field.
No one embraced him, or even waved.

He thought his mother had died, but she
was hanging laundry. He didn't remember

the farmstead being so shabby, the house
nothing but a hut sided with loose planks.

No one offered him a drink of water or tea.
They didn't offer him a chair after his

long journey, or ask him to stay for supper.
What choice did he have but to leave?

He wanted to see what was left, if anything,
of the nearby village. Before he walked away

he caught a glimpse of a boy that he thought
must be his lost son Zdzislaw sitting high in

the pear tree. When Tadek was ten he
perched just like his son in the same tree.

Patrimony

He loved me. Wanted to harden me
so I'd survive in the dark forests of Poland.

He cuffed me, beat me with belts;
reveled in his rich command

of Polish insults and swears.
He had a sixth-grade education,

but he'd earned his wisdom.
Just ask his mother who blessed him

with her death when he was nine.
Ask his father whose razor strop tutored him

until knowledge bled from his wounds.
Ask his first wife, his darling Stefka,

who gifted him her death at 21
birthing a stillborn daughter.

Ask the *kapos* in the Nazi labor camp
who kissed him with whips, pipes,

cudgels, and their fists. Ask the men
who'd died in his labor camp because

they hadn't been hardened enough by love,
unlike my father, to survive the war.

Taking Out the Trash: TWO

I take out the trash before going to bed. My father
is standing under the street light. He's wearing

khaki pants and flannel shirt, ready for yard work.
Over thirty years since he died. He says he still

can't sleep, so he walks everywhere. He says
Poland is a different country now. He's learned,

finally, to speak English. He'd like to step inside
my house. Maybe meet my family. There's much

he wants to say. I tell him I was never brave enough
to father children. Liz is upstairs; I won't wake her.

But we can sit in the kitchen and I'll steep
chamomile tea. I have stories to tell him. He says

he's been waiting a long time for this moment.
I lead him up the front stairs and into my house.

Scenes with My Father

Our father fills the pantry
with the abuse he grows

in his garden where the sun
shines day and night.

    *

He walks around the house
spilling kerosene,

then strikes a match
to light a cigarette.

    *

After he dies, his heart
flutters through the house,

perches on the furniture
to trill a sweet melody.

    *

I keep him in his coffin
in the living room,

cover it with a table cloth
when I dine with him.

    *

I return from work
and find father's corpse,

like a pickled herring,
marinating in the bathtub.

    *

I meet a woman, Kasha,
who keeps her mother in a coffin.

I bring my father in his coffin
to meet Kasha and her mother.

*

I hear father whispering
inside his coffin.

Is he talking to me?
To his dead mother?

*

*When he was a boy, nine,
my father saw*

*his mother's corpse laid out
on their kitchen table.*

*

When I read on the sofa
my father sometimes

steps out of his coffin
to lie down next to me.

*

Father and I can sit together
for hours without saying a word,

while our dreams lap on
each other's shores.

ACKNOWLEDGMENTS

First and foremost, I want to thank Judy Delogu for her indispensible commentary about the poems in *Collected Father*.

Special thanks to poets Lloyd Schwartz, Steven Ratiner, Jean Flanagan, and Cathie Desjardins for the generous gift of their time and expertise in reading my poems and discussing them with me.

And a loud thank you to all the members of the Beehive Poetry Group where many of the poems in this book were introduced and discussed.

And, of course, I thank my late mother (Marianna) and father (Tadeusz), who faced untold adversities in early 20th century Poland and during the three years they each spent in Nazi labor camps during World War II. I often asked them questions about their life stories, which they nearly always rebuffed. As I grew older, their desire to share what they'd experienced became more important than maintaining their silence.

I was deeply saddened when I recognized that my mother had internalized her trauma from WW II, just like so many other women who'd been traumatized in their lives. She became withdrawn and depressed for much of her life. She deserved better.

My father was a typical male who externalized his trauma through anger. Having been bullied and abused by his father in Poland, and then by those in charge of his Nazi labor camp, he projected his anger at easy targets—his two young sons in America. You might think that a person who'd suffered severe paternal anger and institutional degradation would understand how much damage was caused by such violence, but psychology is rarely this simple. The sad truth is that my father never shed the legacy of his abusers.

I believe that my poems about growing up with a damaged and abusive father are a contribution, however small, to the ever-growing second-generation library of Holocaust literature. Despite our difficulties with our father, compared to what he'd faced in WW II, my brother and I had it easy, however distressing and damaging it may have been for us.

I grew up living in two very different worlds: one created by my parents' experiences in Poland and their years in Nazi labor camps, and the wonder of Boston that offered libraries, museums, education, literature, architecture—a high order of aesthetics. When I stepped out of my parents' house, I was so grateful to be far from everything they had suffered. It took me years to realize that I carried their world with me wherever I went in America. And it was this perspective of two different worlds grafted together that became the source of the poems in *Collected Father*. I was determined to write these poems with a cold, clear, fearless eye, as a matter of history, of humanity.

John Pijewski's parents met and married in a Displaced Persons Camp in Germany after being imprisoned for three years in separate Nazi labor camps during World War II. Together, they spent an additional five years caught up in postwar bureaucracy. They were denied immigration to Brazil, Canada, and Australia before they were allowed to enter the United States as war refugees with their six-month old infant son, Jurek, in November 1950.

John was born in Boston, Massachusetts, in 1952. He graduated from Boston University, the University of New Hampshire in Durham, and attended Iowa's Writers' Workshop.

His book of poems, *Dinner with Uncle Jozef*, was published by Wesleyan University Press in 1982. In 1984 John received a writing fellowship from the National Endowment for the Arts. He taught Creative Writing as an adjunct professor at Boston University, the College of the Holy Cross in Worcester, Massachusetts, and the University of Southern Maine in Portland for over 30 years. At the same time he also restored a handful of 19th century houses in and around Boston, converting them into condominiums. Retired in 2016, John lives in a vintage house in Somerville, Massachusetts.

The poems in *Collected Father* chronicle John's difficult relationship with his father who had been traumatized by his time in a Nazi labor camp, as well as the grinding poverty on a farm in Poland with a father who could've been a character in *The Painted Bird*, Jerzy Kosinski's acclaimed novel of an abandoned boy trying to survive on his own in the brutal peasant culture of Poland during WW II.

John's parents led insulated lives in Boston within a Polish-speaking community. They never learned to speak or read English, or drive a car. Although they lived in America, it was as if they'd never left Poland.

www.ingramcontent.com/pod-product-compliance
Lightning Source LLC
Chambersburg PA
CBHW031435150426
43191CB00006B/528